Contemporary Collection

For Piano Students

Revised Edition

Contents

Project Manager: Judi Gowe Bagnato
Cover Design: Martha Ramirez

© 2001, 1963 Summy-Birchard Music
a division of Summy-Birchard Inc.
Exclusive print rights administered by
Alfred Music Publishing Co., Inc.
All Rights Reserved. Printed in USA

ISBN 0-87487-627-3

The Shepherd Plays

Andante cantabile

T. Salutrinskaya

Sitting Beside a River

Avraham Sternklar

Autumn Song

Andante

Dmitri Kabalevsky, Op. 39, No. 11

Scherzo on Tenth Avenue

With a steady bounce

David Kraehenbuehl

Festival in Spain

From *Adventures in Style* Book 2

Elvina Pearce

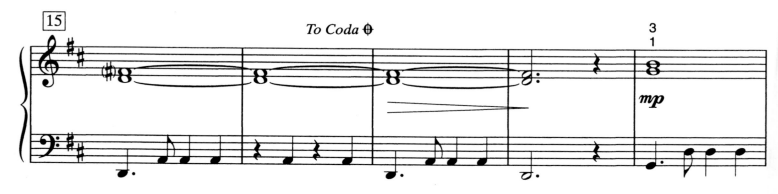

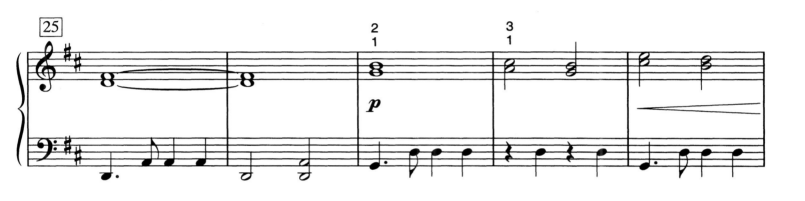

Coda

0627S

Toccata Breve

David Kraehenbuehl

Dream World

David Kraehenbuehl

Slowly and gently

Snowfall

Very slowly and gently

David Kraehenbuehl

The Trail

Lawrence Auguillard

Bells

Fred Ziller

Allegro moderato

Folk Song

Fred Ziller

March

Moderato *very rhythmic, with sharp accents*

Fred Ziller

Dusk

Stanley Fletcher

Whimsical Waltz

Very simply

Stanley Fletcher

Intermezzo

Frederick Koch

Etude in White

Pesante ♩ = 126

David Kraehenbuehl

Half-Asleep

Lynn Freeman Olsen

Lento

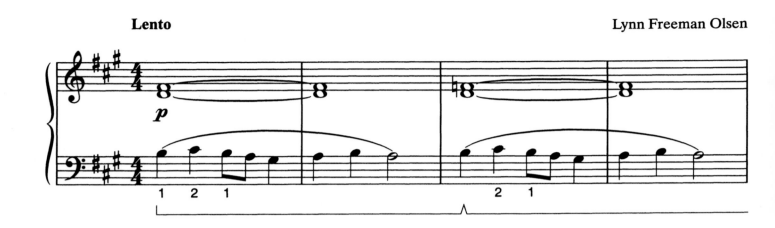

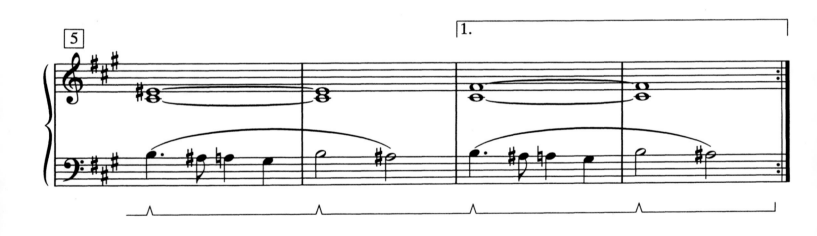

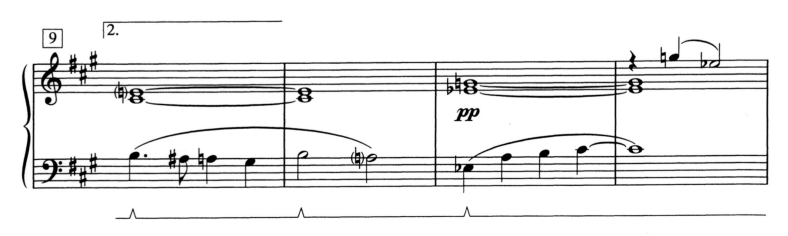

2222222

2222222222

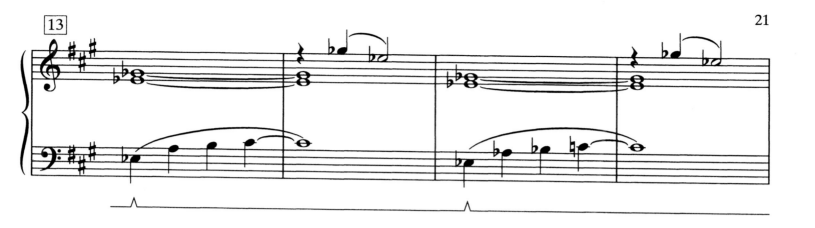

Etude in Blue

David Kraehenbuehl

23

0627S

The Mirror

Moderato ♩ = 56

William Pottebaum

Dirge

Lento ♩ = 42–44

William Pottebaum

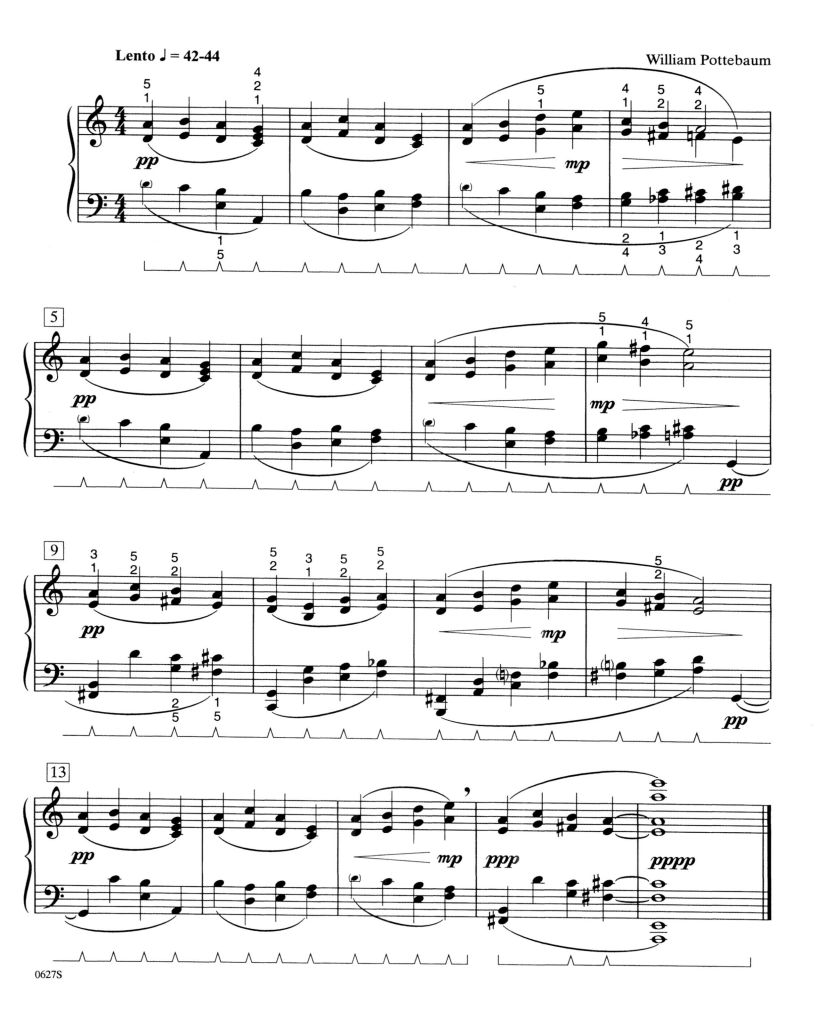

Scherzo

Dennis Riley

Rain

Con brio ♩ = ca. 120

Dennis Riley

2 *l. h. sempre staccato*

Night Shadows

One of the developments in twentieth-century music is the use of a tone row as a basis for composition. The principles of this system were evolved by Arnold Schoenberg. Later composers of serial music have made their own adaptations of these principles.

The row, or series, contains all twelve half steps within the octave. The composer can arrange these tones in any order, but the particular order he chooses becomes the source of his entire composition. The original row may be used in three other ways: It may be inverted (all ascending intervals become descending intervals of the same size, and vice versa). Both the original and inverted rows can occur backwards (retrograde and retrograde inversion). In the row or any variant, the tones must occur in proper sequence, but may be used successively as a theme or simultaneously as harmony. A tone when introduced can be repeated immediately, but cannot be reintroduced until it returns in the sequence.

Night Shadows is based on this original row and two variants:

meas. 1-4, etc.

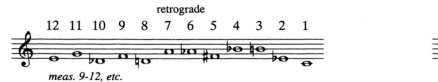

meas. 9-12, etc.

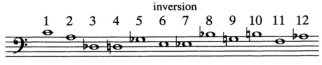

meas. 12-15, etc.

Ihor Bilohrud

Fanfares

Gerald Shapiro

Procession

Norman Auerbach

Siciliana

Moderato ♩ = 48

Robert Keys Clark